"Nevada is the great unknown. A land of incredible beauty, it covers more than a hundred thousand square miles of brilliantly colored terrain rising in chain after chain of mountains. Many of them lift snow caps ten to thirteen thousand feet or ascend to pinnacles sculptured into weird or striking forms."

—*Nevada: A Guide to the Silver State*

OVERLEAF: Cirrus clouds above Sand Mountain at sunrise, Salt Wells Basin.

LEFT: Wind-scoured snow on ridgeline, Desatoya Mountains, Desatoya Mountains Bureau of Land Management Wilderness Study Area. Shoshone and Toiyabe ranges are in the distance.

"Nevada is ten thousand tales of ugliness and beauty, viciousness and virture. 'Old Virginia' Finney stumbles on a rock and smashes his bottle of whisky: 'I baptize this ground Virginia City.' Mark Twain hoaxes and outrages miners with a fake news story of a bloody massacre at Dutch Nick's... Herbert Hoover pulls a twenty-five pound trout from the green waters of Pyramid Lake. General Grant faints in the steam-hot depths of a silver mine: 'This is as near hell as I want to get.'"

—Richard G. Lillard
Desert Challenge: An Interpretation of Nevada

Travertine cones and terraces of Geyser Hot Springs, also know as Fly Geyser, Black Rock Desert.

MAGNIFICENT
WILDERNESS

NEVADA

PHOTOGRAPHY BY **SCOTT T. SMITH**

FOREWORD BY **HAL ROTHMAN**

PUBLISHED BY **WESTCLIFFE PUBLISHERS, INC.**

ENGLEWOOD, COLORADO

EDITOR: *Suzanne Venino*
DESIGNER: *Rebecca Finkel,*
F + P Graphic Design
PRODUCTION MANAGER:
Pattie Coughlin

PHOTOGRAPHS AND TEXT
© 1996 Scott T. Smith
All Rights Reserved
FOREWORD *© 1996 Hal Rothman*
All Rights Reserved

INTERNATIONAL STANDARDS BOOK NUMBER
1-56579-153-3
LIBRARY OF CONGRESS CATALOGUE NUMBER
96-60392

PUBLISHED BY: *Westcliffe Publishers, Inc.*
2650 South Zuni Street
Englewood, Colorado 80110
PRINTED BY: *C&C Offset Printing Co., Ltd.*
Printed in Hong Kong

ACKNOWLEDGMENTS

Thanks to the great people I have met while traveling in Nevada. Ann Kersten and Greg Ebner fed me, supplied maps, and offered much information and advice. Marge Sill sent me a guidebook. I am grateful to the mule skinners and horse packers who served my wife and me chili verde at the trailhead in the dark when we misjudged how long it would take to hike out of the Table Mountain Wilderness. Thank you to the land sailor who gave me a ride for several reaches across the Black Rock Desert, and explained the history of the Burning Man.

Land managers and staffers of the Forest Service, Bureau of Land Management, National Wildlife Refuges and Nevada State Parks were very helpful and friendly.

A special thanks to members of the Friends of Nevada Wilderness and members and staff of the Nature Conservancy for their continuing dedication and determination in the effort to protect Nevada's wild country. Stephen Trimble's book, The Sagebrush Ocean, has been an indispensible reference during my travels through Nevada.

A big thank you to Steve and Linda Kyriopoulos at Sterling Springs Ranch in Cache Valley, Utah, for letting us use their llamas. Our trail buddies Rocket, Wind River, Paulus and Navarone made it easy to get camera and camping gear into the Nevada backcountry.

I am grateful to my parents, Glen and Afton Smith, and Mary's parents, Ben and Arleen Bedingfield, for, among many other things, feeding us and providing a shower and a place to sleep when the drive to or from the wilderness was too long to make in one day.

Thanks to John Fielder, Suzanne Venino, Dianne Howie and the rest of the staff at Westcliffe Publishers for their environmental commitment and for producing great books.

Most of all, I would like to thank my wife, Mary Bedingfieldsmith. She is my key grip, llama wrangler, camp tender, gear carrier and model when she is able to come with me; my office manager, secretary and inspiration when she must stay home. She puts up with my absences, endures my foul moods, and informs me when it is time to stop before I get the truck stuck on bad four-wheel-drive roads.

I dedicate this book to Mary, who doesn't mind waiting for the right light.

TABLE OF CONTENTS

Lake Mead at dusk, view from Devils Cove,
Lake Mead National Recreation Area.

FOREWORD

My first vision of Nevada was at nightfall, crossing from eastern Oregon one summer long ago. Sunset approached with rapidity —one minute it was daylight, the next, night had fallen, first purple and then almost immediately pitch black, the night of the undisturbed desert, with only stars above. The sole source of light on State Highway 140 came from my headlights. Silhouetted against the skyline were the starkest forms of landscape I had ever seen: lines, shapes and features that, even in the dark, defied categorization. These were not the ordinary scary monsters of the night. The images in front of my headlights were far different, far more surreal, yet simultaneously more real than the phantoms that creep at the edges of the night.

More than a decade later, I moved to Nevada and began to relish its many contradictions. Nevada is an anomaly among American states. It contains some of the hottest places in the nation and some of the coldest. Nearly the entire population lives in just two counties; much of the rest of the state is practically uninhabited. Two of Nevada's highways have the moniker of the nation's loneliest road; on Highway 50, in the northern part of the state, it is possible to drive a hundred miles or more without seeing another car. Eighty-seven percent of the state, the seventh largest in the union, is in federal hands, most of which is administered by the Bureau of Land Management (BLM). Though mostly desert, Nevada has more than 8.6 million acres of forest, an area larger than the state of Maryland, but comprising only one-twelfth of Nevada. The oldest living plant in the world, the bristlecone pine, is found in Nevada, as is the nation's only federally designated wild horse range. While most of the state is undeveloped, its revenue is largely derived from urban tourism and gaming. The population is clustered in dense cities on small lots, huddled against the spectacular backdrop of the mountains and the stark, expansive deserts. In the eyes of a newcomer, Nevada was indeed a place of stark contrasts.

To most people, Nevada's natural attributes remain hidden behind the glare that comes from its glittery urbanity. Las Vegas defines the image of the state, with casinos that sell unreality and the ongoing fiction of random prosperity. Yet in the rest of the state there is incredible scenic beauty, a diversity of flora and fauna and an array of topographies and geographies that dazzle even the most seasoned outdoors people. Nevada upsets all conventions about scenic beauty. It twists the expectations of Americans accustomed to a humid-clime landscape.

Rain is the rarest of commodities in Nevada, but when it does rain, the land is transformed. Especially in spring, flowers answer the rare rain with a plethora of colors. Overnight, blossoms erupt, showering the world with brilliant yet transitory colors. It is like finding the end of the rainbow; for a moment, you're awash in radiant color, bathed in its seeming perfection and oblivious to the rest of the world.

In its color, its size and scale, in its scope, Nevada is different than the rest of the nation. Its cacti take many shapes, and its deserts fail to conform to standards of order. Mountains jut unusually, almost eerily, and land forms possess remarkable contours. Much of Nevada's soil harbors spores and desert plants but little of the vegetation to which most Americans are accustomed. The plants that spring from it, with their contorted spires and spines, show again and again how Nevada defies traditional concepts of beauty.

Space—open, lonely, exhilarating space—is another enduring trait of the Silver State. Outside of the Las Vegas metroplex and Washoe County in the north, Nevada seems infinite. Only the horizon and the mountains break the never-ending vistas. Vast expanses rarely see a human being and larger areas are only peripherally traversed. The view from the road is always clear, uncluttered by dense brush, with light and shapes receding to the horizon. Spending time in rural Nevada can feel like living 150 years ago, in a world of fewer people and a more intimidating landscape. It is a hard land that creates a hard people, but in that cultural granite is a rooted existence, intrinsically tied to the places of rural Nevada.

Nevada has long been considered a wasteland, a geographic aberration to cross as quickly as possible. Its land has been preserved and protected by accident, mostly because only a few were willing to brave the hardships necessary to extract its wealth. Difficult to reach and expensive to utilize, Nevada's resources were developed to the extent that was feasible during the great consumptive periods of the late nineteenth and early twentieth centuries. But those capabilities were not great in comparison to the size and diversity of the state, creating a situation where preservation occurred because of inaction rather than action. Too few people and too few companies were willing to invest to conquer this expansive state, leaving a legacy of de facto preservation unequaled anywhere else in the lower forty-eight states. Even the BLM lands, which make up so much of the state, were left to the federal government because homesteaders did not want them and ranchers and miners did not want to keep them. Nevada remained wild because few were willing to brave its extreme nature to attempt to tame it.

In recent years, this uncontested protection has been challenged. In the 1980s and 1990s, groups that advocate local control of natural resources came to the fore in the "cow counties" of rural Nevada. These "sagebrush rebels" constructed a locals-first doctrine that was based largely on the idea of "culture and custom," the supposition that time-honored patterns of behavior on public land conveyed de facto ownership to long-time users. As much wishful thinking as response to an economic climate changing for the worse, this idea had no roots in any statute. Their claim to federal lands in Nevada was fundamentally specious, for the state gave up its lands as a condition of statehood in 1864. Such land was public domain; it was not local land, as sagebrush rebels liked to insist. In the eyes of most Americans, the land was merely "locally located," entrusted to local people until such time as the rest of the nation sought to claim it. The Sagebrush Rebellion precipitated a battle between old and new, urban and rural, tradition and modernity—and it raised the question of de facto protection.

For the overwhelming number of Nevadans the issue produces a range of problems. Nevada fancies itself a place without conventional rules; here the Old West lives on. Yet nearly all Nevadans live in cities, and most seek to have rural lands open for recreation, not closed to all but the locals who live there. Nor is Nevada a wasteland any longer. As the state's population has almost doubled in the past decade, people have come to see Nevada as more than just a blank spot on the map. Their advocacy at first slowed, and now has apparently halted, the siting of the nation's first high-level nuclear waste repository facility in the state. The wasteland analogy is slowly evaporating as America's definition of what constitutes natural beauty changes. As the nation becomes more populated and open spaces more difficult to find, the once intimidating expanse of Nevada has come to signify freedom.

The de facto protection of the past will not last much longer. The growing number of Nevadans and people from other states who want to experience the beauty of Nevada, a beauty portrayed so strikingly in Scott Smith's photographs, have put pressure on the existing arrangements. Nevada is at a crossroads; either more rules will be put forward to manage the increasing flow of people on its rural lands, or those lands will be turned over to individuals and become private preserves. The only certainty is that the status quo, created by the beauty, remoteness and stark austerity of Nevada, will not hold.

— HAL ROTHMAN

HAL ROTHMAN *is Professor of History at the University of Nevada, Las Vegas, and editor of* Environmental History. *He is the author of numerous books and articles about the environment of the American West, including* "I'll Never Fight Fire With My Bare Hands Again": Recollections of the First Forest Rangers of the Inland Northwest *and* On Rims and Ridges: The Los Alamos Area Since 1880. *His work has been featured on the CBS Evening News and in* The New York Times *as well as in numerous other venues.*

PREFACE

Wallace Stegner once noted that to appreciate the scenery of Nevada one had to acquire a new set of values about scenery. Nevada landscapes are more often subtle than ostentatious. To those who define scenery as humid, green countryside, or snow-covered mountains rising above forested lakes, or crashing surf along a coastline, the vast and lonely terrain of Nevada's Great Basin and Mojave Deserts can appear hopelessly bleak and uninspiring. To these people Nevada remains a blank spot in their minds, just one hell of a long, dull drive to get to the surrealism of one of the neon gambling ghettos, or a transit to be endured while traveling to or from California.

Those of us who have stopped to look, who have walked a mountain ridgeline or the edge of a playa, know that this land does not reveal itself all at once. It can be aloof even to those who love it. It may take many miles of driving and hiking before one appreciates the intricate relationship of flora and fauna, the exposed and complex geology, the complicated and compelling beauty of Nevada's wild country. Or it may be love at first sight. The mountains, valleys and plateaus of Nevada are full of splendidly isolated singular places. Here are some of the most remote, least visited, strangest landscapes in the country. I think this is wilderness at its best.

I am an unabashed, unapologetic fan of the Mojave and Great Basin Deserts. I am exhilarated by the distance, the silence, the dryness and clarity of the air. I know the different smells of sagebrush, creosote, or juniper woodland after rain. And I know that in many mountain ranges there are decidedly un-desertlike glacial cirques sheltering summer snowbanks, alpine flowers in wet meadows, and forests on cool, north slopes.

If you drive west from the far eastern edge of the Great Basin (the Wasatch Front, where I was born and raised and now live) you take a roller-coaster ride through a land of pale grays and browns, repeatedly climbing to a pass, descending to a valley—the rhythm of the basin and range country. My first memories of driving west, and of Nevada, come from a trip my family took to Lehman Caves. I don't remember much about the caves, but I do remember a picnic table on a hot slope of brush and scrubby trees. While our parents set out food, my sister and I wandered among nearby trees and made an amazing discovery—real cactus with unreal-looking, impossibly bright magenta flowers. That this could be was a revelation for a six-year-old accustomed to the suburban lawns of Salt Lake City.

Shooting star in bloom at a spring, Monitor Range, Table Mountain Wilderness, Toiyabe National Forest.

Later, when my father took summer classes at UCLA, we made the long drive down Interstate 15 to California, with Las Vegas as an overnight stop. It was a breathtaking experience to step from an air-conditioned car into a one-hundred-degree, neon-lit evening. But what really fascinated me was the new and exotic vegetation I saw through the window as we crossed the desert. Fuzzy-looking cholla cactus; strange, twisted Joshua trees; and creosote bushes on long, shimmering slopes below the baking rock of a low range. And always in the distance were higher mountains hovering above the scrim of heat waves. A formidable and imposing landscape to be sure, but one that seemed to hold the promise of secrets revealed if one were to poke around some.

While going to college, I worked summers on a Bureau of Land Management fire crew based in western Utah. We often found ourselves in Nevada, joining crews from Ely or Elko. Bushwhacking up trailless ridges to a lightning strike with a water pack, or swinging a pulaski while digging fireline on a smoking bajada was hard work, but I was getting paid to hike around in wild country—more than fair compensation. What I saw while doing it was a bonus: young mule deer sparring, eagles bringing rabbits back to young in a cliff-face nest, tiny creeks full of small trout, lupine and paint-brush under the sage, a limestone cave with bats on the ceiling. By the time I graduated, I had fallen completely under the spell of this least written about, least visited, least photographed American landscape.

It is possible in Nevada to have an entire wilderness to yourself. One July, my wife and I packed with llamas into the Alta Toquima Wilderness of Mount Jefferson for a week. We photographed streams and lakes, alpine meadows filled with flowers, cliffs, and conifer forests, scenery not much different, superficially, from the Rockies or the Sierra Nevada. Hiking in, we made the only footprints on the only trail. Hiking out, ours were still the only footprints. If you want even more assurance of a solitary experience, you can try a Bureau of Land Management Wilderness Study Area. You will likely have to drive forty miles on dirt roads to get to a rutted, possibly impassable jeep trail which takes you to the base of a rugged mountain range with no trails. Hiking here it is easy to believe you are the first person to stand on a spot, and you may be. If there is water, the cowboys have been there before you. If there are minerals, the prospectors checked out the area. But several limestone ranges with neither have been labeled by the BLM "interior largely unknown."

Many friends from across the country—and even some people I have talked to in Las Vegas and Reno—are

"All through Nevada the scenery is most forbidding: nothing but vast tracts of sand, and sage-brush, and glittering alkali. Occasionally near the stations there may be a patch of cultivated land, but that will be all."

—J.W. Boddam-Whetham
Western Wanderings: Record of Travel in the Evening Land

amazed when I tell them I am photographing landscapes in Nevada. They can't believe there is anything "out there." I think that perception suits many Nevadans fine. Let the crowds go to the Colorado Plateau, to Yellowstone and Yosemite. We'll savor the solitude and keep this part of the world's secrets to ourselves. It is an attitude I sympathize with even as I show people some of its secrets through my photos. But the belief by many that there is "nothing out there" puts Nevada's wild lands at risk. There is little objection when multinational corporations tear down whole mountains for microscopic gold or when hundreds of square miles are given over to the testing of weapons. Stream banks can be grazed to dust. Thousands of waterfowl disappear when water is diverted and wetlands dry up. The state is perceived to be the perfect place to bury nuclear waste. Philip Hyde, in the introduction his book, *Slickrock,* voices my sentiments well:

> *The focus of this book is on a part of Earth that is still almost as it was before man began to tinker with the land… I have some hesitation in showing more people its delightful beauty—hesitation born of the fear that this place, like so many others of great beauty in our country, might be loved to death, even before being developed to death. So if our book moves you to visit the place yourself sometime, first make sure you add your voice to those seeking its protection.*

Or as writer-photographer Stephen Trimble puts it:

> *If [Congresspeople] have never heard of the Great Basin… when it comes time to ratify the next MX missle system or electronic warfare range proposed for Nevada, we can guess how they will vote. After all, there's nothing out there, is there?*

So put on your boots and hat, stick a water bottle in your knapsack, and take a walk through the Joshua trees below the Mormon Mountains. Climb to the bristlecone pines on Mount Grafton. Fish the basalt gorge of Salmon Falls Creek. Watch the stars come out above the Black Rock Desert. Acquire a "new set of values about scenery" and fall under the spell of Nevada's wilderness. And then add your voice to those who know that its complex terrain and rich ecosystems are worth the struggle for their protection.

—SCOTT T. SMITH

"Whether the visitor comes from the land of summer rains along the Allegheny Mountains or Great Lakes, from the sunny valleys of California, the arid plains of New Mexico, or the interminable plains of British America, the climate of Nevada will puzzle him. Though apparently shut in by a high mountain range on the west which should ward off fierce winds from that quarter, the wind will come pouring down the ravines forty or fifty miles an hour with force enough to sweep everything less in size than bullets into clouds, pelting one exposed to it as if with shot, and sending clouds of dust high into the air or through the closest weatherboarding into the farthest closet or pantry in the house."

—*Thompson & West's History of Nevada*

LEFT: Eroded alkali mud near Carson Lake, Cocoon Mountains are in the distance.

OVERLEAF: Sagebrush on the foothills of the Jarbidge Mountains, Marys River Basin.

"And with Nevada these high, discrete, austere new ranges begin to come in waves, range after range after north-south range, consistently in rhythm with wide flat valleys: basin, range, basin, range; a mile of height between basin and range. Beside the Humboldt you wind around the noses of the mountains, the Humboldt, framed in cottonwood—a sound, substantial, year-round-flowing river, among the largest in the world that fail to reach the sea. It sinks, it disappears, in an evaporite plain, near the bottom of a series of fault blocks that have broken out to form a kind of stairway that you climb to go out of the Basin and Range."

—John McPhee, *Basin and Range*

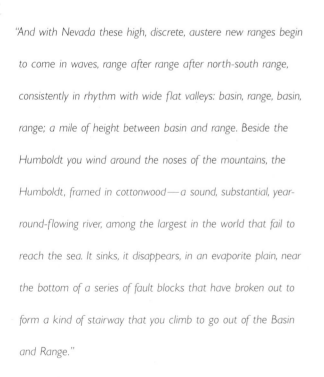

Jeff Davis Peak and aspen at sunset,
Snake Range, Great Basin National Park.

ISLANDS IN THE SKY

We are sitting near the summit of Mount Jefferson in the Alta Toquima Wilderness, looking to the southwest with binoculars, and counting mountain ranges. There are eleven ridgelines, hazy blue cutouts stacked one on top of another. The faintest is that of the lofty White Mountains nearly eighty miles away.

Depending on who is doing the counting, there are somewhere between 150 and 300 separate mountain ranges in Nevada. What *is* certain is that if you climb to a peak in any range and look around you will see other mountains—lots of other mountains. Even in the Owyhee Desert, or around Massacre Lake, where lava flows from the Snake River Plain have buried and smoothed the terrain, there are always mountain ranges on the horizon, beyond the cliffs and plateaus of basalt.

Nearly all of Nevada is in the Basin and Range physiographic province, defined by long, narrow mountain ranges separated by broad, elongated basins. This part of the earth's crust is under tension. It is being pulled apart along an east-west axis, and has fractured into north-south trending blocks. Some of the blocks have sunk, some have been uplifted and tilted. The high parts of the blocks are the mountain ranges, their tilted nature evident in the asymmetric configuration that Nevada ranges usually display, with one steep side, one more gradual side. The spaces between these uplifted blocks form basins, their true depth hidden by thousands of feet of sediment, the debris of eroded mountains. Most Nevada ranges are surrounded by extensive alluvial fans and bajadas; they stand buried to their knees, or waists, or shoulders in their own detritus.

We may not be able to enumerate them exactly, but each range has a unique character determined by a combination of geology, elevation, latitude and its own endemic mix of plants and animals. Like islands in the sky, they form a vast archipelago that sweeps across the state. These mountains do not reveal their character immediately. I find my best photographs are made after I have hiked a range, after I have spent some time poking around its canyons and looking out from a peak or a ridge. Only then does it begin to share its secrets.

Lush vegetation along Goshute Creek, Cherry Creek Mountains, Goshute Canyon Bureau of Land Management Wilderness Study Area.

ABOVE: Spruce trees below cliffs and patches of summer snow in
a glacial cirque, Snake Range, Great Basin National Park.

OPPOSITE: Autumn snow on Piper Peak in the
Silver Peak Range, view from Fish Lake Valley.

"The typical Great Basin mountain range tilts: it has one relatively gentle slope, one side that rises abruptly from the desert floor. It is narrow—not over 15 miles across—and long—50 miles or more. Rugged canyons dissect it. Rarely are there 'foothills,' only the lower slopes of an uninterrupted ascent. Rock type varies. Toward the west edge of the Great Basin, granite predominates; dolomite, a relative of limestone, is common toward the east. Volcanic rocks occur throughout but cover thousands of square miles in the north."

—John Hart, *Hiking the Great Basin*

OPPOSITE: Wind-scoured snow on ridge below Mt. Rose, Carson Range, Mt. Rose Wilderness, Toiyabe National Forest. Lake Tahoe Basin is in the distance.

LEFT: Volcanic boulders and brush on the crest of the Desatoya Mountains, Desatoya Mountains Bureau of Land Management Wilderness Study Area.

" *Mountain lions and bighorn still live in the Snake Range. Here you sit before a stage just after the curtain rises for the next act but before the players enter. Life is poised to act, suspense, magic.*

"*This same feeling of wholeness is the reason one need not visit a wilderness to value it. Its existence can change your reality, your awareness of options. Always you know you can retreat to such a place, a possibility that opens up the the frontiers of consciousness.*"

—Stephen Trimble, *The Sagebrush Ocean, A Natural History of the Great Basin*

OPPOSITE: Tracks of snowshoe hare on ridge above
Lee Canyon, Spring Mountains, Toiyabe National Forest.

LEFT: Aspen in autumn below Jeff Davis Peak, Snake Range,
Great Basin National Park.

ABOVE: Aspen on Table Mountain, Monitor Range,
Table Mountain Wilderness, Toiyabe National Forest.

OPPOSITE: Aspen on ridge below cirrus clouds, Table Mountain,
Monitor Range, Table Mountain Wilderness, Toiyabe National Forest.

"Suddenly we topped the ridge, and I halted to gaze breathlessly at the view before me. Ranges of mountains, towering one over another, marched away into the distance until the last was only a grey-blue film. Hundreds of feet below us lay the central spot of the roundup, with the familiar brown mass in the center and the distance between filled with curved lines of mountain and plain for miles and miles in every direction. The effect on me was staggering. I thought of every significant line of outdoor poetry I had ever encountered. The only one that echoed in my memory now with realization, was Henry Van Dyke's line from 'God of the Open Air':

> Oh, how the sight of the things
> that are great enlarges the eyes!

"The vastness, the eternal quiet, the beingness! Here again no green appeared except the dull grey-green of the sage in the foreground, but tan and brown and lavender, pink and those wonderful pastel blues that shade off into grey."

—Mrs. Hugh Brown, *Lady in Boomtown*

Paintbrush on ridge above Morgan Pass, Goshute Range. View from Bluebell Bureau of Land Management Wilderness Study Area into Goshute Peak Wilderness Study Area.

"We christened our camp 'Kievea Nee-niet,' or the 'Mountain Spring,' and declared we would spend a whole month in this delightful place....Before us, to the northward, miles on miles away, lay spread out the most magnificent panorama of mountain scenery ever seen or conceived of... I could not convey... more than a faint, uncertain notion of that appearance of lightness, yet overwhelming conviction of massiveness and solidity, observed and felt in standing before those mountains, and those hills that skip and roll at their feet!"

—Dan DeQuille, *Washoe Rambles*

False hellebore rings tarn in glacial cirque. Toquima Range.
Alta Toquima Wilderness, Toiyabe National Forest.

October snow near the summit of Wheeler Peak,
Snake Range, Great Basin National Park.

Limber pine at sunrise, Toquima Range,
Alta Toquima Wilderness, Toiyabe National Forest.

"The wagon trail aims directly at Pilot Peak of the

Pilot Range, which we could see clearly, upward of fifty

miles away—a pyramidal summit with cloud coming

off it in the wind like a banner unfurling. Across the dry

lakebed, the emigrants homed on Pilot Peak, standing

in what is now Nevada, above ten thousand feet. Along

the fault scarp, at the base of Pilot Peak, are cold

springs. When the emigrants arrived at the springs,

their tongues were bloody and black."

—John McPhee, *Basin and Range*

ABOVE: Pilot Peak rises above a playa
on the Utah-Nevada border.

OPPOSITE: Lichen on volcanic rock, Fang Ridge,
Reveille Range, Reveille Range Bureau of Land
Management Wilderness Study Area.

"We soon rose from Pine Valley by a long, irregular, generally moderate ascent to a mountain divide, from which our trail took abruptly down the wildest and worst canyon I ever saw traversed by a carriage. It is in places barely wide enough at bottom for a wagon, and if two should meet here it is scarcely possible that they should pass. The length of the canyon is a mile and a half; the descent hardly less than two thousand feet; the side of the road next to the watercourse often far lower than the other; the roadbed is often made of sharp-edged fragments of broken rock, hard enough to stand on, harder still to hold back on. The heat in this canyon on a summer afternoon is intense, the sun being able to enter it while the wind is not. Two or three glorious springs afford partial consolation to the weary, thirsty traveler. I am confident no passenger ever rode down this rocky ladder; I trust that none will until a better road is made here, though a good road in such a gulch is scarcely possible."

—Horace Greeley, *An Overland Journey from New York to San Francisco in the Summer of 1859*

Moon above basalt cliffs, Little High Rock Canyon, Little High Rock Canyon Bureau of Land Management Wilderness Study Area.

"This Nevada terrain is not corrugated, like the folded Appalachians,

like a tubal air mattress, like a rippled potato chip. This is not—

in that compressive manner—a ridge-and-valley situation. Each

range here is like a warship standing on its own, and the Great

Basin is an ocean of loose sediment with these mountain ranges

standing in it as if they were members of a fleet without prece-

dent, assembled at Guam to assault Japan."

—John McPhee, *Basin and Range*

Moon and Lake Peak at sunset, Ruby Mountains,
Ruby Mountains Wilderness, Humboldt National Forest.

"For the next one hundred and forty miles [from Pleasant Valley] or thereabouts, our trail led us mainly up one side of a mountain range and down the other, thence across a valley of some ten miles in width to the foot of another chain, and so on. As the train naturally runs up the deepest canyons and over the lowest passes, the ascent and descent are rarely abrupt for any considerable distance, and we seldom lacked water; but our route was the most devious imaginable——veering from northeast on one hand to south on the other. Sometimes, two or three hundred square miles were visible at a glance.... "

—Horace Greeley, *An Overland Journey from New York to San Francisco in the Summer of 1859*

OPPOSITE: Limber pine snags, East Humboldt Range, East Humboldt Wilderness, Humboldt National Forest.

LEFT: Bunchgrass and juniper snag on slope above Pleasant Valley, Tobin Range, Tobin Range Bureau of Land Management Wilderness Study Area.

Joshua trees and Lime Ridge, Lime Ridge
Bureau of Land Management Wilderness Study Area.

"The enveloping space is as beautiful as it is simple. The whole vertical landscape is there, unchanged since Fremont's day except for the man-sized gopher holes called prospect tunnels... At a colossal right angle to it, the horizontal landscape, farmed along the drainage bottoms, cut by a meandering road or two. The broad sweep of flood plains, the abrupt gorges that head them, the purple, crested ranges that curve out of sight. The cycloramas of cosmic blue above. The clean spicy air that a thunderstorm blows down from a sagebrush mesa.... On summer evenings the full moon is a luminous continent. Mark Twain would recognize it all as he would the ocher-colored buttes, the greasewood-covered mud flats, and the flocks of gawking sage hens along the side roads between ranches and prospectors' camps. The Ruby Range is as lonely, its glacial lakes as quiet, and the foxtail pines of the Toiyabe Mountains are as lovely and untouched as when John Muir tramped the timberline zone and munched on dried raisins and chocolate bars."

—Richard G. Lillard
Desert Challenge: An Interpretation of Nevada

LEFT: Volcanic butte near the crest of the Goshute Range, Bluebell Bureau of Land Management Wilderness Study Area.

OVERLEAF: Sagebrush and grasses in Morgan Basin, foothills of the Goshute Range, Bluebell Bureau of Land Management Wilderness Study Area.

"The patterns of ecological communities in the Great Basin change constantly, and the current version is a recent innovation, decisively different from most times in its history. I sit in a camp chair in Stone Cabin Valley and try to comprehend this fact. Mountains surround me—the Kawich Range, gray-blue and craggy to the southeast, the Hot Creek Range, closer and rich in detail to the northeast, behind me the Monitor Range. The air is still and hot, and time seems indolent—the present the length of forever. I scrunch my toes in coarse gravel—bits of the mountains on the horizon brought down into the valley by millions of storms during millions of summers."

—Stephen Trimble, *The Sagebrush Ocean,*
A Natural History of the Great Basin

OPPOSITE: Boulder above North Twin River drainage, Toiyabe Range, Arc Dome Wilderness, Toiyabe National Forest.

LEFT: Lichen on cliff in the Santa Rosa Range. Granite Peak is in the distance.

RIGHT: Barrel cactus above Arrow Canyon, Arrow Canyon Range, Arrow Canyon Range Bureau of Land Management Wilderness Study Area.

OPPOSITE: Frozen pothole in sandstone, Spring Mountains, Red Rock Canyon National Conservation Area, LaMadre Mountains Bureau of Land Management Wilderness Study Area.

"We interact with the nature of each range. For example, so much life exists in the lush Ruby Mountains that our visits have little effect on their spirit. So many organisms blossom and crowd and compete and clatter about here that a human presence is imperceptible. The Rubies go about their business, neither requiring nor bestowing acknowledgment."

—Stephen Trimble, *The Sagebrush Ocean,*
A Natural History of the Great Basin

OPPOSITE: View of North Furlong Lake and the Ruby Mountains from the summit of Wines Peak, Ruby Mountains Wilderness, Humboldt National Forest.

LEFT: Buckwheat and phlox above Stewart Creek drainage, Toiyabe Range, Arc Dome Wilderness, Toiyabe National Forest.

BETWEEN THE MOUNTAINS

As I walk farther and farther out onto the cracked, alkali mud of the playa in Railroad Valley, the distances expand. The surrounding mountains recede, seeming to duck below the curvature of the earth. The sky becomes a vast, hot, blue dome, clamped down tightly around the horizon. Yet, even as I have the impression of shrinking in the landscape, I feel more significant, more singular. In the middle of a Nevada basin it is easy to feel that I am standing at the center of the universe.

Most of Nevada drains internally. Except for the Owyhee River and its tributaries, which flow north into the Snake River, and the White River, Meadow Valley Wash and Las Vegas Valley drainages, which empty into the Colorado River in the southeast corner of the state, the state's creeks and rivers have no outlet to the sea. A typical basin feature is a gleaming alkali flat, the seasonally wet dead end of a closed drainage system. Many of these basins held large lakes only twelve to fifteen thousand years ago. Pyramid and Walker Lakes are remnants of the largest of these, Lake Lahontan.

The basins are the home of the deliberate desert tortoise and the speedy pronghorn. Here grow the brushes and bushes: sagebrush, rabbitbrush, saltbush, creosote bush. When rain falls in the right amount at the right time, sere valleys in the Mojave Desert burst into unlikely color as annual wildflowers bloom in profusion. Sand dunes grow at the feet of mountain ranges where the wind drops grains gathered from ancient lake beds. Here, between the mountains, are the rare desert wetlands and their remarkable concentrations of wildlife.

A strong December wind hissed through the sagebrush of the Goshute Valley as I attempted to photograph drifting snow. Giving up, I turned to watch an approaching snow squall obscure the Pequop Range. As the snowflakes thickened and the cold wind drew tears from my eyes, I would not have been at all surprised to see a mammoth emerge from the white, pursued by Pleistocene hunters clad in animal skins gesturing for me to join them. Nevada's basins can do that to you.

Patterns in ice, Cathedral Gorge,
Cathedral Gorge State Park.

"We were now about to leave the valley of the great southern branch of the Columbia river, to which the absence of timber, and the scarcity of water, give the appearance of a desert, to enter a mountainous region where the soil is good, and in which the face of the country is covered with nutritious grasses, and dense forest —land embracing many varieties of trees peculiar to the country, and on which the timber exhibits a luxuriance of growth unknown to the eastern part of the continent and to Europe. This mountainous region connects itself in the southward and westward with the elevated country belonging to the Cascade or California range; and, as will be remarked in the course of the narrative, forms the eastern limit of the fertile and timbered lands along the desert and mountainous region included within the Great Basin—a term which I apply to the intermediate region between the Rocky Mountains and the next range, containing many lakes, with their own system of rivers and creeks (of which the Great Salt is the principal), and which have no connexion with the ocean, or the great rivers which flow into it. This Great Basin is yet to be adequately explored. And here, on quitting the banks of a sterile river, to enter on arable mountains, the remark may be made, that, on this western slope of our continent the usual order or distribution of good and bad soil is often reversed; the river and creek bottoms being often sterile, and darkened with the gloomy and barren artemisia; while the mountain is often fertile, and covered with rich grass, pleasant to the eye, and good for flocks and herds."

—John C. Fremont
October 13, 1843, Report of the Exploring Expedition to the Rocky Mountains in the Year 1842 and to Oregon and North California in the Years 1843-1844

Eroded sediments and cirrus cloud at dusk.
Cathedral Gorge State Park.

"On the nineteenth day we crossed the Great American Desert—
forty memorable miles of bottomless sand, into which the coach
wheels sunk from six inches to a foot. We worked our passage
most of the way across. That is to say, we got out and walked.
It was a dreary pull and a long and thirsty one, for we had no
water. From one extremity of this desert to the other, the road
was white with the bones of oxen and horses. It would hardly be
an exaggeration to say that we could have walked the forty miles
and set our feet on a bone at every step! The desert was one
prodigious graveyard. And the log-chains, wagon tyres, and rotting
wrecks of vehicles were almost as thick as the bones."

—Mark Twain, *Roughing It*

Cocoon Mountains and Carson Sink
at sunrise, Salt Wells Basin.

"The hinterland of Nevada is a country of far horizons broken only by mountain barriers lost in the haze of distance, and unexpected green valleys that break upon the traveler's eye with the breathstopping impact of a mirage. They are meandering belts of greenery where giant cottonwoods and quaking aspen and fragile willows line the banks of streams and rivers that are as precious as gold in this land of little rain. Here, away from factories and pollution, the air is so clear that objects leap into view from miles away. A rock formation on a faraway rim of a hill becomes a pebble that one could reach out and pick up between his fingertips."

—Robert Laxalt, *Nevada: A Bicentennial History*

LEFT: Prehistoric petroglyphs on sandstone, Valley of Fire State Park.

OVERLEAF: Joshua Trees near St. Thomas Gap, Virgin Mountains are in the distance.

Brush below Pilot Range at sunset, Tecoma Valley.

"Sometimes on a winter's night when the wind moans through the high trees and snow spatters against the windowpanes, and lights are low and the rustling fire in the grate suffuses the room with a warm glow, and home becomes a cave against the storm and I think about Nevada...

"I think of a soft northern desert that stretches from horizon to horizon without intrusion by man. In fact, there is not a single tree to impede my vision. The only movement is the stirring of the topmost tips of sagebrush in the breeze of late afternoon, and high above, the silent soaring of an eagle with his white tail feathers spread out in a fan."

—Robert Laxalt
Nevada: A Bicentennial History

Brittlebush and sandstone, Valley of Fire State Park.

"Geologic processes of uplift and erosion are in a dynamic tug of war here. Mountains are young and still rising. Shorelines of deep lakes etch the valley slopes, now burning with desert drought. Titanic forces have been locked in massive conflict. The inexorable upward pressure from heat imbalances in the earth's interior has been countered by the destructive leveling power of water and ice. The unceasing struggle between these basic elements, fire and water, has created the grandeur of the terrain."

—Bill Fiero
Geology of the Great Basin

Prehistoric petroglyphs on basalt, Grimes Point.

Wild horses in the Ralston Valley.

"...the Great Basin Desert has a past-finished aspect, as if all that could be done to it has been done, and now it is old and tired and worn-out, grizzled and gutted, faded and weather-beaten. Sometimes the land has a worn velvet look, tucked with arroyos, pleated with mountains, a landscape seemingly without seasons or eternally halfpast autumn, a landscape left out to dry, forgotten, tattered with rain, wrinkled with sun, and yet, in a peculiar sense I cannot explain, always vital and never forlorn."

—Ann Haymond Zwinger
The Mysterious Lands

Nest and eggs of killdeer, Black Rock Desert, Black Rock Desert
Bureau of Land Management Wilderness Study Area

"The train whistles past the Utah-Nevada border. Less than five hundred miles to go. At the open window, the sky is brilliantly blue, and the ceaseless pulse of the wind seems to bring the familiar dry, pungent smell of sage and dust. Mornin' on the desert and the air is like a wine, and it seems like all creation has been made for me and mine. There is a sense of boundless space. Whole cities could be lifted from the East and set down in the declivity between one peak and the next, only to diminish to the proportions of anthills in this infinitude. But there are no cities, just a few towns, scarcely glimpsed before they pass. Men have not stayed long nor mattered much. This desert has scarcely altered in a thousand years, yet it constantly changes with the shifting play of color and light. Cloud shadows meet and part on the gray sand like fish swimming in a transparent sea. As the sun slips down from the meridian, the western mountains darken from gentian to slate to a velvety indigo blue, while the eastern range warms from gray to mauve to mulberry. Pools of dark shadow fade to gauze, rocks turn luminous, and the sharply cut canyons dissolve in a rosy mist."

—Sally Springmeyer Zanjani
The Unspiked Rail: Memoir of a Nevada Rebel

LEFT: Ranch above Pyramid Lake in autumn, Pyramid Lake Indian Reservation.

OVERLEAF: Fresh snow in Spring Valley below the Schell Creek Range.

"The argument whether or not Sand Mountain had crossed

the highway made more sense when I saw the thing—a single

massive mound of tawny sand, a wavy hump between two larger

ridges of sage and rock. It was of such a size that, while it wasn't

perhaps big enough to be a mountain by everybody's definition,

it was surely more than a dune."

—William Least Heat Moon
Blue Highways: A Journey into America

RIGHT: Thunderstorm over the Reese River Valley.
View from the Arc Dome Wilderness, Toiyabe Range.

OPPOSITE: Rippled dune at Sand Mountain,
Cocoon Mountains and Carson Sink are in the distance.

Rabbitbrush in bloom on bajada below Fortification Range. Spring Valley and Snake Range are in the distance.

"These valleys are bigger than you ever remember, and so are the mountains that bound them, each one popping up sequentially from below the horizon—a landmark. The basins feel more like oceanic fjords (temporarily dry) than valleys. There appears to be nothing in them, just a low growth of black sage and grass, with less conspicuous plants next to the playas. Every few miles a grove of cottonwoods and poplars up against the foot of the range marks a ranch, situated where the creeks flowing from the mountains can be tapped before they dissipate in the basin. And here and there a mining operation makes raw the mouth of a canyon. Nothing else. That's all."

—Stephen Trimble, *The Sagebrush Ocean,*
A Natural History of the Great Basin

Eroded sediments and cirrus cloud,
Cathedral Gorge State Park.

"From here [Great Salt Lake] Fremont sent…myself to cross the

desert, which I have often heard had never before been crossed

by white men. Old trappers would speak of the impossibility of

crossing it, saying that water could not be found, nor grass for

the animals…. We traveled about sixty miles, found neither

water nor grass, nor a particle of vegetation, with the ground as

level and bare as a barn floor, before we struck the mountains

on the west side of the lake. There we found water and grass

in abundance….

"We passed over a fine country, abounding in wood, grass, and

water, having only about forty miles to travel without water before

reaching the [Walker] Lake."

—Kit Carson, *Kit Carson's Autobiography*

RIGHT: Joshua trees at dusk, foothills of the Mormon Mountains, Mormon Mountains Bureau of Land Management Wilderness Study Area.

OPPOSITE: Joshua trees on slopes below the Mormon Mountains, Mormon Mountains Bureau of Land Management Wilderness Study Area.

"The country from Battle Mountain to Austin is the most genuine western country you can imagine. You see there some of the genuine ranches and real Cow-boys. The country is nothing but alkali and sage brush but cattle live on it. The land is wonderfully rich, but too dry for crops. The trip from Battle Mountain…is up a valley between two ranges of mountains which get higher as you approach Austin…. Mr. Stokes' Tower is about half a mile from the town on the face of one of the mountains. The view from there is beautiful. We can see up and down the valley for a great distance and across to the next range, a distance of about 60 miles. I don't know of any place of its kind anywhere. It is very romantic in every way and the most ideal place to live in I can imagine. The air is simply delightful and the climate is as fine as any that can be found."

—Tasker L. Oddie
February 10, 1898, Austin, Nevada,
Letters from the Nevada Frontier:
Correspondence of Tasker L. Oddie, 1898-1902

Wildflowers in Pahrump Valley after a wet winter.

"Empty landscape like the Black Rock playa seems somehow to pay attention to the entrance of a human. Each of us makes a difference; we make the land more alive. We feel a change in the reality of the place because we are there."

—Stephen Trimble, *The Sagebrush Ocean,*
A Natural History of the Great Basin

Salt-encrusted mud below the Jackson Mountains,
Black Rock Desert, Black Rock Desert Bureau of
Land Management Wilderness Study Area.

"Humans like rhythm. And sand dunes are rhythmic, their

winding S-curves moving back and forth with the wind,

alternating lee side and slip face, light and shadow.

"Their smoothness is striking—even playas are marked by

mudcracks. But smooth sand in larger dunes in the Great

Basin contrasts with the spiny surrounding shadscale. Smooth

and feminine curves of sand; angular and masculine shrubs."

—Stephen Trimble, *The Sagebrush Ocean,*
A Natural History of the Great Basin

OPPOSITE: Sand dune and Bloody Run Peak, Winnemucca Dunes,
Little Humboldt River Valley.

LEFT: Cross-bedded sandstone, Valley of Fire State Park.

"On the huge playa [of the Black Rock Desert], I camped far

from 'shore.' What seemed awesome became comprehensible

through simplicity. The size of the playa made me feel small,

yet no visible living thing separated me from the mountains

forty miles away, a realization that created intimacy. The playa

disoriented because nothing gave it scale—no plants, no birds,

no lizards, not even rocks. Mosquitoes, a wasp, a dragonfly

nearby made little difference. I was alone."

—Stephen Trimble, *The Sagebrush Ocean,*
A Natural History of the Great Basin

RIGHT: Cracked mud surface of the playa, Black Rock Desert.

OPPOSITE: Early winter snow and blackbrush,
Gabbs Valley. Gabbs Valley Range is in the distance.

WATER IN AN ARID LAND

It is the duty of any outdoor photographer to seek out and sit in as many hot springs as possible. Because it is so rare there, lovers of the desert have great affection for water; naturally hot water in which you can immerse yourself has a special appeal. In Nevada, where the earth's crust is stretched thin and her internal heat is not far below the surface, you can visit places named Hot Creek, Warm Springs, Caliente, Thousand Springs, and many others where hot water finds its way to the surface.

All water is enormously important in Nevada, where less precipitation falls than in any other state. But it's not as arid as many imagine. After all, as dendrologist Ronald Lanner notes, "Why, this is the Great Basin Desert, and it is practically full of big, friendly mountains that catch the snow and use it to grow forests and meadow flowers." The mountains also use it to feed creeks and streams. Melting snow recharges the aquifers that rejuvenate the springs on hillsides and in valleys and supply the groundwater that is pumped for irrigation and drinking.

Water in the desert is a powerful attractor. Nevada's towns and cities are built near water. Where a perennial creek emerges from a mountain range, you will more than likely find a ranch using that water to grow cows and hay. Millions are drawn to the reservoirs on the Colorado River, their boats skimming sparkling waters incongruous with the backdrop of calescent rock. The Humboldt River, the only true river that Nevada can claim as solely her own, was the main route west for pioneers headed to California and Oregon.

Animals are also drawn to water. Riparian (streamside) vegetation has importance far out of proportion to the tiny area it occupies. This habitat is critical for a large percentage of Nevada's wildlife. Marshes like Ruby Lake and Stillwater are crucial stopover and nesting areas for water birds on the western flyway.

Sitting up to my chin in a warm pool near Soldier Meadows I think about a wetter Nevada. I imagine a vast lake, an arm of which once occupied this valley. Lake Lahontan covered much of northwest Nevada during the Pleistocene epoch. If it existed today, it would extend more than 250 miles, from McDermitt to Hawthorne. Pyramid and Walker Lakes are remnant puddles of that ancient lake. Both continue to shrink, the rivers that feed them diverted. Pyramid Lake once overflowed into Winnemucca Lake. In 1924, fishermen there still floated boats and caught perch. By 1938 Lake Winnemucca had dried up.

As hot water flows around me, I wonder how many more of Nevada's wetlands might suffer the same fate before they are recognized as the extraordinary natural systems they are.

Detail of frozen pothole in sandstone, Red Rock Canyon,
LaMadre Mountains Bureau of Land Management Wilderness Study Area.

"Most of Nevada lies within the Great Basin—a depression whose floor is scored by numerous mountain ranges trending north-south and lying athwart the natural east-west flow of travel. With a few exceptions in the extreme northern and southern parts, all rivers draining its 110,690 square miles flow into sinks and lakes within the State.... The largest streams are the Humboldt, crossing northern Nevada from east to west, traversing deep gorges cut into the north-south ranges crossing its course; in the western section the Carson, now emptying into Lahontan Reservoir; the Walker, rising like the Carson and Truckee, in California, and emptying into Walker Lake, which lies along the eastern flank of the Wassuk Range; and the Truckee, fed by Lake Tahoe and flowing into Pyramid Lake in Washoe County. . ."

—*Nevada: A Guide to the Silver State*

Greys Lake, East Humboldt Range, East Humboldt Wilderness, Humboldt National Forest.

"The next morning on the desert I was awakened by the squeal

of seagulls. I looked out the window. I should have been used to

the vagaries of the desert, but I wasn't. Sure enough, a pair of

gulls overhead."

—William Least Heat Moon
Blue Highways: A Journey into America

RIGHT: Boulders and ice in South Fork Owyhee River, South Fork
Owyhee River Bureau of Land Management Wilderness Study Area.

OPPOSITE: Goose Lake and the Stillwater Range,
Stillwater National Wildlife Refuge.

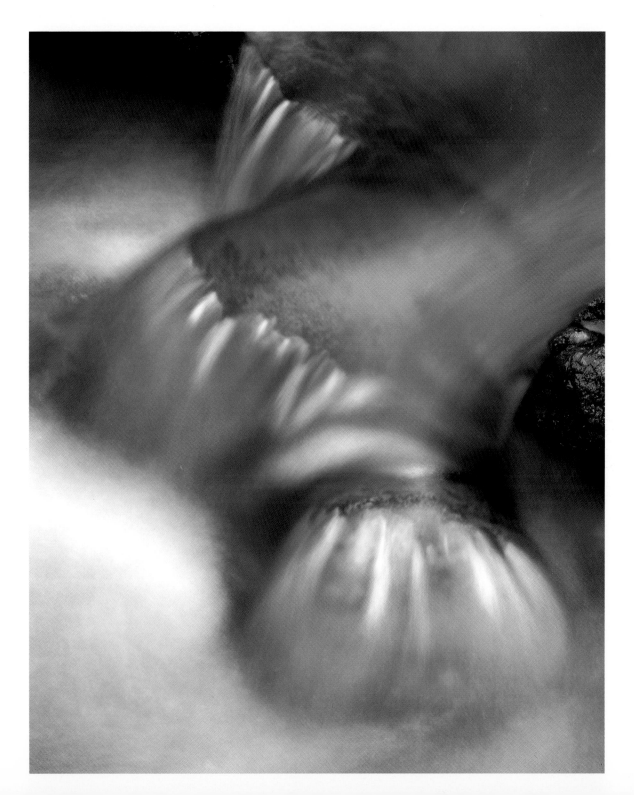

"At dawn a luminous golden glow began to shine just north of Horseshoe Bend where the dark, blue Pine Nut Hills dipped low. The water birds wheeling high above the reservoir glinted white as snowflakes when the first beams caught the rock tips of the sage-furred hills beside the lake. They sifted down to alight on the glassy water or the sanded shore, dotted with clumps of willow bushes, then rose again with a joyous cacophony. White, water-smoothed boulders lay scattered like a herd of sheep on the grassy slope where the stream gurgled cheerfully past the flank of Springmeyer Peak; the west wind swept down from the Sierra; eagles soared above the rocky mesa to the west."

—Sally Springmeyer Zanjani
The Unspiked Rail: Memoir of a Nevada Rebel

LEFT: Small falls along North Furlong Creek, Ruby Mountains, Ruby Mountains Wilderness, Humboldt National Forest.

OPPOSITE: Small falls along Cottonwood Creek, Monitor Range, Table Mountain Wilderness, Toiyabe National Forest.

"At the border of the Desert lies Carson Lake, or the 'Sink' of the Carson, a shallow, melancholy sheet of water some eighty or a hundred miles in circumference. Carson River empties into it and is lost—sinks mysteriously into the earth and never appears in the light of the sun again—for the lake has no outlet whatever.

"There are several rivers in Nevada, and they all have this mysterious fate. They end in various lakes or 'sinks,' and that is the last of them. Carson Lake, Humboldt Lake, Walker Lake, Mono Lake, are all great sheets of water without any visible outlet. Water is always flowing into them; none is ever seen to flow out of them, and yet they remain always level full, neither receding nor overflowing. What they do with their surplus is only known to the Creator."

—Mark Twain, *Roughing It*

OPPOSITE: Cottonwoods and Washoe Lake in winter, Washoe Lake State Park.

LEFT: Willow and creek in McGill Canyon, Jackson Mountains, South Jackson Mountains Bureau of Land Management Wilderness Study Area.

Pyramid Lake at dawn, Pyramid Lake Indian Reservation.

"From Virginia City I went to Carson, where there are some famous hot-springs, said to be a certain cure for rheumatism. All the springs have wonderful legends and stories attached to them. Hot-springs are numerous in Nevada, and are utilised in various ways, some families dispensing altogether with patent stoves and doing all their cooking by means of a domestic geyser."

—J.W. Boddam-Wetham
Western Wandering: A Record of Travel
in the Evening Land

Boulder in Lake Mead at sunrise,
Lake Mead National Recreation Area.

"…we encamped on the shore, opposite a very remarkable rock in the lake, which had attracted our attention for many miles. It rose, according to our estimate, 600 feet above the water; and, from the point we viewed it, presented a pretty exact outline of the great pyramid of Cheops."

—John Charles Fremont
The Exploring Expedition to the
Rocky Mountains, January 14, 1844

RIGHT: Breaking waves on a windy day, Lake Mead,
Lake Mead National Recreation Area.

OPPOSITE: The Pyramid and other tufa formations,
Pyramid Lake, Pyramid Lake Indian Reservation.

OVERLEAF: Mount Grant rises above Walker Lake.

ABOVE: Baker Lake and Pyramid Peak at sunset,
Snake Range, Great Basin National Park.

OPPOSITE: Goose Lake at sunset, Stillwater National Wildlife Refuge.

"But the seasons remain untouched by man. Autumn…when the evening sky is streaked with long, uncertain bands of red, and the dry, rich scent of first fallen leaves is almost painful in its sweetness. Lakes and ponds that gleam like hand mirrors in the dusk, so that the reflection of a golden Collie running along their banks is confused in the still water with the gold of drooping willows."

—Robert Laxalt
Nevada: A Bicentennial History

Barrel cactus above Lake Mead, Devils Cove,
Lake Mead National Recreation Area.

"Along Hendrys Creek on Mount Moriah in the Snake Range, I walked up the canyon, always in aspen, always with the rushing creek. The sound stayed with me for two days, the constant churn of water tumbling down to the desert. When I hiked above it past the spring where the creek starts, the silence startled me. Only when I did not hear the stream did I realize how my ears had adapted to it."

—Stephen Trimble, *The Sagebrush Ocean,*
A Natural History of the Great Basin

Salmon Falls Creek emerges from basalt gorge,
Badlands Bureau of Land Management Wilderness Study Area.

"This morning we continued our journey along this beautiful

stream, which we naturally called the Salmon Trout River [Truckee].

Large trails led up on either side; the stream was handsomely

timbered with large cottonwoods; and the waters were very

clear and pure. We were travelling along the mountains of the

great Sierra, which rose on our right, covered with snow; but

below the temperature was mild and pleasant."

—John Charles Fremont
The Exploring Expedition to the
Rocky Mountains, January 16, 1844

Headwaters of Pine Creek, Toquima Range,
Alta Toquima Wilderness, Toiyabe National Forest.

"Our supply of water was gone… I became uneasy…. When he [my partner] arrived he was so eloquent in praise of a spring he had found some two miles up the cañon that I was determined to visit it and have at least one good drink from it…. We reached the spring, very much heated and very thirsty, and not daring to drink at first, bathed our hands and faces in the cool, limpid stream at a spot where it poured over a ledge of rocks. This spring bursts out on the side of a steep mountain some three hundred feet above the cañon and comes tumbling down over the rocks and among a tangled mat of grass and trailing vines and water plants that form a beautiful veil which hangs from the mountain's brow. The water of this spring rises through the sandstone formation and, being thus filtered, is by far the purest and sweetest water I have tasted in this Territory."

—Dan DeQuille
Washoe Rambles

Waterfall and wildflowers, cirque above Angel Lake,
East Humboldt Range, Humboldt National Forest.

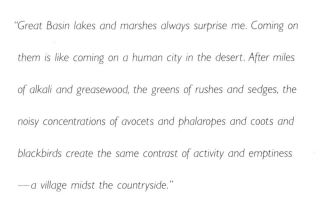

"Great Basin lakes and marshes always surprise me. Coming on them is like coming on a human city in the desert. After miles of alkali and greasewood, the greens of rushes and sedges, the noisy concentrations of avocets and phalaropes and coots and blackbirds create the same contrast of activity and emptiness —a village midst the countryside."

—Stephen Trimble, *The Sagebrush Ocean, A Natural History of the Great BAsin*

RIGHT: Small falls along Stewart Creek, Toiyabe Range, Arc Dome Wilderness, Toiyabe National Forest.

OPPOSITE: Marys River emerges from the Jarbidge Mountains.

"I...stood for a while looking at the landscape [Tonopah]
—line upon line of running color, tan, henna, lavender, brown.
But no green. Not a tree. Not a shrub. A faint odor floated by
me reminiscent of Christmas, a spicy something I afterward
recognized as sage.

"I had been born in San Francisco, had lived all my life in the
green fragrance of that moisture-laden air, and yet this dry,
rarified atmosphere, so sparkling, this vast expanse of open
country were overpoweringly lovely."

—Mrs. Hugh Brown
Lady in Boomtown

OPPOSITE: Rabbitbrush on basalt above Salmon Falls Creek,
Badlands Bureau of Land Management Wilderness Study Area.

LEFT: Ice in the South Fork Owyhee River, South Fork Owyhee
River Bureau of Land Management Wilderness Study Area.

"We plodded on…and at last the Lake [Tahoe] burst upon us— a noble sheet of blue water lifted six thousand three hundred feet above the level of the sea, and walled in by a rim of snow-clad mountain peaks that towered aloft full three thousand feet higher still! It was a vast oval, and one would have to use up eighty or a hundred good miles in traveling around it. As it lay there with the shadows of the mountains brilliantly photographed upon its still surface I thought it must surely be the fairest picture the whole earth affords."

—Mark Twain, *Roughing It*

"Three months of camp life on Lake Tahoe would restore an Egyptian mummy to his pristine vigor, and give him an appetite like an alligator….The air up there in the clouds is very pure and fine, bracing and delicious. And why shouldn't it be?— it is the same the angels breathe."

—Mark Twain, *Roughing It*

OPPOSITE: View of Lake Tahoe from Carson Range, Mount Rose Wilderness, Toiyabe National Forest.

LEFT: Lake Mead at dusk. View from Garrett Buttes Bureau of Land Management Wilderness Study Area.

ANNUALS AND ANCIENTS

It had been a wet winter in southern Nevada. In April, I photographed the annual desert wildflowers making unabashed displays of color around the Muddy Mountains. A dry wash was splashed with color as purple phacelia, orange globemallow, yellow desertgold, and pale primrose grew in clusters and shoals. Along a limestone ledge was a whole row of rare golden bearpaw poppies. It was a spectacular exhibition by plants that may lie dormant as seeds for years until the right combination of precipitation and temperature triggers germination and the race to grow, flower and set seed before the moisture is gone.

Nevada has an extraordinary diversity of plant communities. Biogeographers (the scientists who study what species live where, and why) find the state to be remarkably dynamic and complex. We can make a crude simplification and correlate living communities with elevation. The low valleys in the southern part of the state lie within the Mojave Desert, with its characteristic creosote bush, Joshua tree, yuccas, chollas and periodically prolific annuals. Further north, in the Great Basin Desert, shadscale covers the lowest basins, with salt-tolerant plants like greasewood rimming the playas. Above that grows sagebrush, a species so ubiquitous that for many it symbolizes the Great Basin. With more elevation and precipitation comes the "pygmy forest" of pinyon and juniper trees. Higher still is a zone of mountain brush, which is dominated by sagebrush and mountain mahogany, with groves of aspen. In the Rockies or the Sierra Nevada, pine and fir would grow at this elevation, but in most Nevada ranges these trees are absent. The highest peaks have open groves of limber and bristlecone pine, giving way to alpine tundra.

But this description is a broad generalization greatly complicated by details. Bunch grasses are a significant component of the sagebrush steppe of the Owyhee Desert. Pinyon pine disappears from the pinyon-juniper woodland north of the Humboldt River. Whitebark pine is virtually the only conifer in the Ruby Mountains, subalpine fir the only one in the Jarbidge Range. Species common to the Sierra Nevada are found around Lake Tahoe and in several ranges in the western part of the state. Eastern ranges support Rocky Mountain flora, with ponderosa and whitebark pine, white fir, Douglas fir and Engelmann spruce forming a more diverse forest. Nevada's complex ecological mosaic can dazzle and confuse.

We are eating lunch high on the flank of Mount Grafton. Growing out of a crack in the dolomite slab that is our seat is a young bristlecone pine, maybe four inches tall. A bristlecone pine more than 4,500 years old was found across the valley in the Snake Range. In the warm autumn sun, it feels like it might be nice to take root, to watch the world from one perspective for a while. Nevada's natural communities are dynamic. We wonder what changes we might see if we watch with this little tree for the next four millennia.

Bristlecone pine cones and paintbrush, Snake Range, Great Basin National Park.

"…I stopped at a wayside set back in a box canyon of

wet juniper and sage. The scent of plants saturated the mist.

Alexander the Great, I've heard, was preserved in honey, Lord

Nelson in brandy, and Jesus in aloe and myrrh. If I can choose,

I'll take my eternity in essence of sage and juniper."

—William Least Heat Moon
Blue Highways: A Journey into America

Snow on prickly pear cactus, Red Rock Canyon, LaMadre
Mountains Bureau of Land Management Wilderness Study Area.

"Not only were the flats and lower parts of the hills thus luxuri-
antly clothed in bunch grass and red-tops, but the tallest peaks
were green to their very summits. There appeared to be a most
generous flow of moisture rising by capillary attraction through
the stratified sandstone formation and oozing out in a fertilizing
sweat from base to apex of all the surrounding hills. There was
grass — green, waving dewy grass, above, below and around us
— verily a world of grass!"

—Dan DeQuille, *Washoe Rambles*

Mountain ash and aspen, riparian vegetation in
Thomas Canyon, Ruby Mountains, Ruby Mountains
Wilderness, Humboldt National Forest.

"Compared to the huge aspen forests of Colorado, New Mexico, and central Utah, Great Basin stands are puny. But in the ocean of desert shrubs and tough little woodland trees that surround them, these few aspen bring a rare touch of brightness and luxuriance to the Basin mountains. Even the most hard-bitten prospector gentles when passing through the white-trunked glens of trembling-leaved aspen."

—Stephen Trimble, *The Sagebrush Ocean*
A Natural History of the Great Basin

Aspen leaves and spruce cones and needles on metamorphic rock, Snake Range, Great Basin National Park.

"…I opened the envelope. With the unsealing came the unleashing of a forgotten scent that struck me like a physical force.

"Hidden between the pages was a single sprig of Nevada sagebrush. Before I could protect myself, the memories were summoned up and washed over me in a flood. They all had to do with sagebrush.

"Sagebrush that rolled over the vast plateaus and brutal desert mountains like an endless gray sea, ringing the few scattered hamlets and towns of Nevada so that they were like islands in that sea. Sagebrush growing down to the banks of rare streams and rivers so that water seemed to be captive in a bigger sea. Sagebrush giving up its domain only when it reached the foothills of the western Sierra where deep forests of pine and fir and tamarack ruled supreme.

(continued on next page)

Aspen leaves along North Creek, Schell Creek Range, Mount Grafton Bureau of Land Management Wilderness Study Area.

(continued from previous page)

"Sagebrush in the spring with the tender tips of first growth mingling with the gray. Sagebrush in summer when the blazing sun made the scent almost unbearably pungent. Sagebrush after a spring rain when that scent was muted to the heady fragrance of wine. Sagebrush in the autumn when golden pods burst into puffs at the mere touch of a hand. Sagebrush in the winter, hooded white with snow so that walking through it was like walking through a gnome forest.

"The smell of a sagebrush cookfire at dusk in a desert hollow that was bedground for our sheep, shaggy sheepdogs resting in its light and warmth, and the indistinct figure of my father saying that sagebrush made the hottest cookfire one could ask for."

—Robert Laxalt
Nevada: A Bicentennial History

Narrowleaf cottonwoods along Hendrys Creek, Snake Range,
Mount Moriah Wilderness, Humboldt National Forest.

"U.S. Highway 50, roller-coastering across the basins and ranges,

rises into pinyon-juniper woodland, drops back into sagebrush,

then plunges on even lower to salt deserts. Up the next pass,

through the woodland again, past bands of mountain brush

and open forest to within sight of the bare mountaintops: alpine

tundra. These basic patterns are undeniable."

—Stephen Trimble, *The Sagebrush Ocean,*
A Natural History of the Great Basin

Subalpine fir, Jarbidge Mountains,
Jarbidge Wilderness, Humboldt National Forest.

[approaching Carson Pass]

"Of course, no trees but evergreens can live—a very few small quaking aspens in the bottoms of the ravines scarcely form an exception—while almost every rood is covered by giant, glorious pines. I saw sugar and yellow pines at least eight feet in diameter and tall in proportion; I am assured that one was recently cut near this road which measured eight feet across at a height of eighty feet from the ground, and from which two hundred and forty thousand shingles were made. Besides these universal pines, there are giant cedars, balsam firs, and some redwood... I never saw anything like so much nor so good timber in the course of any seventy-five miles' travel as I saw in crossing the Sierra Nevada."

—Horace Greeley
*An Overland Journey from New York to
San Francisco in the Summer of 1859*

Incense cedar and ponderosa pines
on shore of Lake Tahoe, Lake Tahoe State Park.

ABOVE: Lupine after summer rain, Toquima Range,
Alta Toquima Wilderness, Toiyabe National Forest.

OPPOSITE: Lupine, Jarbidge Mountains,
Jarbidge Wilderness, Humboldt National Forest.

"Annuals grow, flower, and set seed in the wet season, escaping the worst of the desert, the dry season, as tough seeds. They produce many seeds in a long-evolved compromise with the seed-eating ants, rodents, and birds; each uneaten seed germinates when it reaches its threshold of moisture and warmth, perhaps years after it fell to earth. It races to complete flowering and fruiting, risking a late snowstorm or a heat spell."

—Stephen Trimble, *The Sagebrush Ocean,*
A Natural History of the Great Basin

Lupine and sagebrush, Jarbidge Mountains,
Jarbidge Wilderness, Humboldt National Forest.

"...the mountainsides half covered with cedar and pine, with some dwarf-willows and rose bushes often fringing their slender rivulets, but not a tree other than evergreen in sight. There is a large, pine-leaved shrub or small tree which a driver termed a mountain mahogany and a passenger called a red haw, growing sparingly among the evergreens on some mountain slopes, which seems about halfway between a thornbush and an untrimmed appletree, but nothing else deciduous above the size of a dwarf willow. Even the sagebrush and greasewood appear to be evergreens. Grass is here not abundant but unfailing, as it must be where water is perennial and wood in fair supply."

—Horace Greeley
*An Overland Journey from New York
to San Francisco in the Summer of 1859*

Lupine, mules ears, sagebrush and aspen, Jarbidge Mountains,
Jarbidge Wilderness, Humboldt National Forest.

"It was February and we had left the spring well advanced in California; but in Nevada it was still winter, and the columns of these majestic trees [cottonwoods], golden in the winter sun, were a brilliant contrast to the flat, tan country through which we traveled."

—Mrs. Hugh Brown
Lady in Boomtown

OPPOSITE: Fresh snow on ponderosa pines, Carson Range, Lake Tahoe State Park.

LEFT: Juniper needles and berries, and lichen on volcanic rock, Pancake Range, The Wall Bureau of Land Management Wilderness Study Area

"Arid Nevada is a phrase used only by those who do not know the State. Meadows so densely covered with wild iris that they resemble lakes, roadsides banked with the native wild peach in a display that rivals Washington's famed cherry blossoms, late snowfields splashed with the brilliant red of snowplant, mountain trails almost obscured by the profusion of blue lupine, red Indian paintbrush and wild rose, deserts aflame with the bloom of cactus—this is the true Nevada."

—*Nevada: A Guide to the Silver State*

OPPOSITE: Aspen and spruce trees, Schell Creek Range, Mount Grafton Bureau of Land Management Wilderness Study Area.

LEFT: Bearpaw poppy, Lake Mead National Recreation Area.

"In this ocean of sagebrush, pinyon pines and junipers form the

only dependable woods, the only widespread forest community.

These two trees rarely grow taller than twenty feet—a scale

comprehensible to humans. They twist into singular shapes, stand

in isolated dignity, or grow in dense and friendly concentrations.

Covering more than seventeen million acres, dwarfing in area if

not in stature the patches of full-sized pines, spruce, and fir that

reign on the highest mountains, the Basin pinyon-juniper 'pygmy'

woodland needs no apologia."

—Stephen Trimble, *The Sagebrush Ocean,*
A Natural History of the Great Basin

OPPOSITE: Asters on sandstone, Valley of Fire State Park.

LEFT: Limber pine snags, Toiyabe Range, Arc Dome Wilderness,
Toiyabe National Forest.

"I had previously seen some beautiful valleys, but I place none
of these ahead of Carson....originally a grand meadow, the
home of the deer and the antelope, is nearly inclosed by high
mountains, down which, especially from the north and west,
come innumerable rivulets, leaping and dancing on their way
to form or join the Carson."

—Horace Greeley
*An Overland Journey from New York
to San Francisco in the Summer of 1859*

RIGHT: Bulrushes, Ruby Lake National Wildlife Refuge.

OPPOSITE: Cottonwoods along Carson River.

"The mountainsides along highway 50 west of Ely were shot through with abandoned mining tunnels, the low entrances propped open by sagging timbers; they were the kind of old-time mines that Walter Brennan might come limping out of, chortling his crazy laugh. Magpies, looking like crows dressed for a costume party, swooped from fencepost to post and flicked wings in the mist. The highway was a long, silver streak of wet. Up into the Pancake Mountains, driving, driving, wishing the day would dry off—after all, this was the desert. But the sky remained dark as dusk.

"I looked out the side window. For an instant, I thought the desert looked back. Against the glass a reflection of an opaque face. I couldn't take my attention from that presence that was mostly an absence."

—William Least Heat Moon
Blue Highways: A Journey into America

Paintbrush, Cherry Creek Range, Goshute Canyon
Bureau of Land Management Wilderness Study Area.

"*The Great Basin Desert's youth is startling. Think of it this way: a single ancient bristlecone pine, more than forty-five hundred years old, has lived through the entire span of what we might call the modern biological world of the Great Basin. It has lived twice as long as what we call the modern historical world. And it still lives.*"

—Stephen Trimble, *The Sagebrush Ocean,*
A Natural History of the Great Basin

Wind-blasted limber pine, Snake Range,
Great Basin National Park.

"In the east a faint green glow told us sunrise was not too far

off. . . .The air was filled with the smell of burning cottonwood.

The odor was like incense, and I was enchanted. Through all my

desert years and even today, when I smell burning cottonwood,

I am back in that early morning when I stepped out of the shack

hotel at Hawthorne."

—Mrs. Hugh Brown, *Lady in Boomtown*

RIGHT: Hymenoxys in bloom on tundra, Toiyabe Range,
Arc Dome Wilderness, Toiyabe National Forest.

OPPOSITE: Aspen at dawn, Monitor Range,
Table Mountain Wilderness, Toiyabe National Forest.

RIGHT: Raindrop on columbine, Toquima Range,
Alta Toquima Wilderness, Toiyabe National Forest.

OPPOSITE: Checkerspot butterfly on western groundsel,
High Rock Canyon, High Rock Canyon Bureau of Land
Management Wilderness Study Area.

"The sand for the Winnemucca dune field probably blew east from an old delta of the Humboldt River, made when it flowed farther northwest than it does now. To reach the dunes we make our way across a burned-out area a year or two old, bountiful with annuals — evening primroses, gilias, white-stem evening stars, desert dandelions, buckwheats, tidytips, the tiny blue phlox flowers set in woolly bracts, and lots of alfalfa. The luxuriance contrasts with both the bleakness of the freshly-burned areas and the unburned dune sites where the plant cover is simpler in species, supporting mostly cheatgrass with big sagebrush and rabbit brush. What annuals there are in recent burns are stunted compared to the numbers and kinds in older burned-out patches."

—Ann Haymond Zwinger
The Mysterious Lands

Wildflowers in wash, Muddy Mountains, Muddy Mountains
Bureau of Land Management Wilderness Study Area.

Bumblebee on wild iris, Monitor Range,
Table Mountain Wilderness, Toiyabe National Forest.

"During those years [1870s], while Carson Valley became a fine community, Long Valley stayed half wild. It was a place where sage, juniper, squaw bush, pine nut, and wild peach outnumbered the cabbages; coyotes howled by night in the hills that circled the little valley; jack rabbits darted jerkily from beneath the sagebrush; flocks of hungry deer drifted down from the high country in the spring; and the wind blew harder than it ever blows in the Carson Valley. Nor has it greatly changed today."

—Sally Springmeyer Zanjani
The Unspiked Rail: Memoir of a Nevada Rebel

RIGHT: Detail of barrel cactus, Million Hills, Million Hills Bureau of Land Management Wilderness Study Area.

OPPSOITE: Wild geranium and black cottonwood, Jarbidge Mountain, Jarbidge Wilderness, Humboldt National Forest.

Mountain ranges rise behind Joshua trees and yucca.
Garrett Buttes Bureau of Land Management Wilderness Study Area.

TECHNICAL INFORMATION

The photographs for this book were made primarily with a Toyo 4x5-inch field camera and lenses varying in length from 75mm to 360mm. Canon 35mm cameras and lenses were used for long telephoto shots and some closeups. Panoramas were shot with an Art Panorama back on the Toyo camera. All but two shots were made on a tripod. Exposures were calculated with a Gossen light meter for the 4x5 work and with in-camera meters for the 35mm. Fujichrome Velvia professional transparency film was used for all 4x5 images, Velvia 120 for the panoramic shots. Velvia and Ektachrome Lumiere were used for the 35mm work. The only filters used were a polarizer and a graduated neutral density filter.

SOURCES

Boddam-Whetham, J.W.
Western Wanderings: A Record of Travel in the Evening Land. London: Richard Bentley and Son, 1874.

Brown, Mrs. Hugh
Lady in Boomtown: Miners and Manners on the Nevada Frontier. Palo Alto: American West Publishing Company, 1968.

Carson, Kit
Kit Carson's Autobiography. Milo Milton Quaife, editor. Chicago: R.R. Donnelley, 1935.

DeQuille, Dan (William Wright)
Washoe Rambles. Los Angeles: Westernlore Press, 1963.

Fiero, Bill
Geology of the Great Basin. Reno: University of Nevada Press, 1986.

Frémont, John
The Exploring Expedition to the Rocky Mountains. Introduction by Herman J. Viola and Ralph E. Ehrenberg. Washington, D.C.: Smithsonian Institute Press, 1988.

Greeley, Horace
An Overland Journey from New York to San Francisco in the Summer of 1859. Charles T. Duncan, editor. New York: Alfred A. Knopf, 1964.

Hart, John
Hiking the Great Basin. San Francisco: Sierra Club Books, 1991.

Heat Moon, William Least
Blue Highways: A Journey into America. Boston: Little, Brown & Company, 1982.

Laxalt, Robert
Nevada: A Bicentennial History. New York: W.W. Norton, 1977.

Lillard, Richard G.
Desert Challenge: An Interpretation of Nevada. New York: Alfred A. Knopf, 1942.

McPhee, John
Basin and Range. New York: Farrar, Straus, Giroux, 1981.

Nevada: A Guide to the Silver State. Portland, Portland, Oregon: Binfords & Mort, 1940.

Oddie, Tasker L.
Letters from the Nevada Frontier: Correspondence of Tasker L. Oddie, 1898-1902. William A. Douglass and Robert A. Nylen, editors. Norman: Univ. of Oklahoma Press, 1992.

Thompson and West's History of Nevada: 1881. Berkeley: Howell-North, 1958.

Trimble, Stephen
The Sagebrush Ocean, A Natural History of the Great Basin. Reno, Nevada: University of Nevada Press, 1989.

Twain, Mark
The Works of Mark Twain, Vol. II: Roughing It. Harriet Elinor Smith and Edgar Marquess Branch, editors. Berkley, California: University of California Press, 1993.

Zanjani, Sally Springmeyer
The Unspiked Rail: A Memoir of a Nevada Rebel. Reno: University of Nevada Press, 1981.

Zwinger, Ann Haymond
The Mysterious Lands. New York: Truman Talley Books/Plume, 1989.